FOR DAD

You were an incredible example of what a husband, father, brother, friend and neighbor could be. You were there for me at the beginning of my life, I for the end of yours. I'm proud to have been your first child and live each day with a humble appreciation for all you did to make me the man I am today.

Chris, Thank you for your friendship!

Randy

1

"Leadership By Example And Other Terrible Ideas"

Mister Robinson   8

There's No Such Thing As A Free Lunch   15

John Phillip Sousa   21

Act 1, Scene 1   24

Children Of The Corn   28

Hitting The Wall, Literally!   31

Party Line   36

You Can't Keep The Coffee Full   40

No Punch In The Punch Bowl   44

Janitor By Day, Leader By Night   49

I Think I Can, I Think I Can, I Know I Can!   52

When It's Time To Say You Were Wrong   58

Where's The Dress?   63

Come On Man!   70

Preface

This book captures formative experiences spanning five decades in the workforce beginning as a teenager, through a four-year stint in the Navy, 21-years at Citibank and then 14-years in the hospitality business. When speaking to university classes, I frequently say I'm not an "expert", but rather I have "experience." I believe those who claim expertise are not unlike those who have passed. The dates on a tombstone reflect the end, just as todays date on the calendar represents a new beginning. To me expertise represents past tense, experience represents present.

Even now, in semi-retirement as a "Food Ambassador" at Avera-McKennan Hospital in Sioux Falls, I continue to learn. Someone once said "treat the Janitor as if he were the CEO." If nothing else surfaces in this book in terms of my philosophy of leadership, this one phrase may have said it all. In fact, as you'll read later, I lived those exact words a decade ago.

This book will not in any way comment on political or social figureheads of the past or present. I'm not qualified to scrutinize any of the "leaders" history has given us. There are a myriad set of leadership examples which could be held up, now under the scrutiny of history, as incredibly bad, yes even terrible styles.

I've always been a student of the "*what might have been*." Not in a glass half-full way, merely a person who believes in a series of tipping points which occur on a daily basis in our lives, our friendships, relationships, the country and throughout the world.

This is a topic I covered with some degree of focus in my novel, entitled "*She Said, "One"*", which was published in 2012. I'll leave the forensic review of the capabilities, successes and failures of past leaders to others.

The instances portrayed in pages to follow are real-life experiences where I have first person knowledge. I've done my best to remember and articulate what happened. It's safe to say the ease of recollection increases my belief the events were indelible and formative.

As I write this book, I've come to the conclusion it will be the first in a series. For a couple of reasons. First, I've got more to tell! Second, I know there are hundreds of leaders within my sphere of contacts, associates, and friends who will also easily recall valuable experiences they've had in the workforce worthy of sharing. Therefore, future editions of "**Leadership By Example And Other Terrible Ideas,**" will be collaborative efforts.

During my Citibank years I was exposed to some of the best minds in the world. I relished the opportunity to stand on stage in St. Louis with W. Edwards Deming, a legend in process engineering and creator of the famous "*red beads.*"

I participated in a business-wide Total Quality Management (TQM) movement, ran an employee suggestion program with over 20,000 participants, later provided communication of business successes and opportunities to the same audience, and helped launch the most successful partner card in the history of credit cards (The American Airlines Citi AAdvantage Card).

Through a twist of fate, and because I took a quantum leap of faith, I had the unique opportunity to help create a restaurant "empire" that withstood market forces, a recession and intensive competition to survive and thrive. My years in the hospitality business were filled each day with customer interactions.

I enjoyed experiences like this one at Callaway's. *"Randy, the Chili doesn't have enough beef in it."* Upon receiving this feedback, and in many other instances throughout the years, I would then go directly to those involved and immediately solve the gap between expectation and reality. For better chili, I walked directly to the kitchen, looked at the chili, agreed with the customer and then asked Nick Rerick to ensure the chili got beefier! Real time responsiveness, real time awareness.

Inspiration to write this book came from an instance near the end of my hospitality career when I was making the evening rounds at Foleys, one of the restaurants I operated, along with my business partner, Tim Olson. The property was experiencing a surge in business associated with the holidays.

Part of my "lead by example" style was to jump in, clear tables, do what I could do to assist. It was shortly after I participated full speed for around 10 minutes, one of our incredible servers, Chris Wiggins said *"That's what I love about you RD, you jump right in. You lead by example."* I instantly responded, in the presence of Chris's co-worker, Shelly Morgan, *"as long as the example is good!"* How true!

If you are like me, you've conducted a considerable number of interviews for management positions. It goes without fail a question similar to this will be posed, *"Describe your management style."* More times than not, your candidate will answer *"I like to lead by example."* Now this sounds just peachy doesn't it? Well, unless you are able to do a Vulcan mind meld like Spock and get a glimpse of the past several years of performance, this response could in fact be a major red flag.

Like the example I gave about myself, what does that really mean? Who taught them to be a leader? What decisions did they make affecting critical outcomes? Needless to say, drilling down on these responses is vital. Probing, open ended questions are a must. In the end, only you can judge whether their leadership by example style would be an asset to you and your organization.

History has shown me several extremely qualified candidates who joined our company with experience simply didn't have what it took to be true leaders. Or their styles, either self-learned or taught, were so out of whack with the businesses core values they didn't have a chance at succeeding without a complete re-boot.

In following pages, I'll expose myself as fallible. The experiences I share will occasionally include names. Other examples will not either out of respect, or because I'm not able to remember, or research with accuracy, those involved.

When names are named, I will be telling the story to the best of my abilities and within parameters of memory. Naturally over a 40-year plus span, there could be hundreds of experiences to be shared. I've picked out ones having the most impact, and therefore the most remembered.

The lessons I've learned, and opinions I have, are intended to assist others in running companies, leading teams or for those hoping to chase their own dreams. While several examples of management detailed in the book took place a while ago, the underlying story and outcomes can easily be transferred to today.

As for the art on the front cover of this book, it's a logo created for me by Tom Molstad. Tom is incredibly gifted and took input related to what I would like my "Bell Cow Consulting, LLC," logo to look like. It didn't take many drafts to provide what you see in print. Why Bell Cow? Well, "back in the day," farmers had a cow bell tied around a cow whose primary intent was to lead the other cows back to be milked.

As I brainstormed this book, future speaking opportunities and perhaps consulting, I couldn't help but think there was probably a time in the past when a bell cow also lead the herd into a truck versus the barn!

Mister Robinson

I've decided to start this book at the beginning of my working life as the foundational experiences I had then serve as the basis of my leadership style today. Not including this past history would be like saying Sunday school takes no role in forging religious beliefs and values in adults.

Work is work and its affects and impacts are immune to age. As an employer, I took particular pride in shaping values and behaviors of young employees. Showing up on time, dressing within guidelines, participating on a team, and a host of other elements of daily operations, were all key attributes to our collective success.

My work life began shortly after my father Doug, to whom this book is dedicated, accepted a transfer to southwestern Minnesota while in the employ of "Land O'Lakes", a company he gave his talents to for nearly 35 years. I was born in Valley City, North Dakota and called that community home until the summer following completion of 7th grade.

It was at this time our father accepted a new challenge within the company and chose to make Lake Benton, Minnesota home. It was this move which provided me an opportunity to work virtually non-stop from my 8th grade year through graduation from High School. It was in this small town, with a population of approximately 750 at the time, in which the beliefs and leadership styles I have today were planted.

It's also where I learned, now upon reflection, why "leading by example," can truly be a remarkably interesting idea with each outcome resting on a razor thin margin between victory and defeat.

Life in Lake Benton was certainly quaint. We lived on an acre of land, on the lake, with a southwesterly view of the community. On nights when the lake became calm and laid like glass, lights would appear to stretch nearly to the shore adjacent to our property. As the oldest of five, I may have been the one most impacted by our move from a larger community in Valley City, to the rural setting of Lake Benton.

While it was exciting to move, residing on a lake outside of town seemed at the time to be a death sentence. In Valley City, I had cousins and the ability to ride my bike unimpeded all over. Now, I was five miles from town and isolated. In retrospect, I wish I owned that house now as it was a little slice of paradise. Unappreciated at the time was the fact the move to a smaller community also afforded me several opportunities for employment and earning spending money. One of the first paid jobs I had was working for our closest neighbor, Mister Robinson.

The Robinson's were a modest family. Included in their operations was a farm located approximately four miles to the east, between Lake Benton and Tyler, Minnesota. It was here I received early exposure to leading by example being a terrible idea. I have vivid memories, over 40 years later of the story I'll share.

I can also still remember the smells of the barns I cleaned, the taste of the whole milk we drank, straight from the cooler, and Mister Robinson's penchant for cooking a noon lunch, which while looking incredibly unappealing, always tasted good.

I can't remember if I was 13 or 14 on the day in question. I do remember trees without leaves and a gray sky. There were multiple lessons being shared simultaneously which in itself can be confusing. First, and foremost, was how to operate the tractor. I can't remember the brand, but I do remember it didn't have a cab and I was sitting on the fender as he operated it. He showed me the pedals and levers necessary to ensure safe operations. For those of you who grew up in cities, it may seem strange that those of us who grew up in rural settings learned how to drive tractors before we learned to drive cars, but it is true.

There was also a certain amount of accomplishment I felt having been a recent "city" transplant, that I was about to operate a tractor on my own. Future work done on the farm would include operating a four-bottom plow and spreading manure.

(Okay, I have to share this side story! Mister Robinson and I were out in a field one day towing a tank full of manure. As we moved through the field, you could hear the power take off, or PTO, begin to struggle. It was clear something was wrong on the other end. On this occasion, he was riding the fender, while I drove. He instructed me to come to a stop. He dismounted and after a very short time,

I heard an audible "swoosh" and the PTO became fully engaged again. Moments later, he came back up virtually covered in pig manure with a big smile on his face. There had been corn stalks in the flow and they clogged the purge of the tank. He wrapped his arms around me so I could participate in the fun. When I close my eyes now, I can still see him and smell that putrid smell!)

The second lesson on that particular day was how to demolish buildings by dropping the front bucket of the tractor on them. During our training, in which he led by example, he pulled the tractor up to a building destined for scrap, lifting the bucket as he approached. As the front tires neared the structure, he would pause, then with the bucket raised he began pulling the applicable hydraulic control arm to lower said metal ram on top of the building, slowly pushing down.

Some memories are just plain etched in your brain and this certainly was one. I distinctly remember hearing creaking, cracking, and groaning as wood, nails and joints began to give way. With a suddenness, the entire structure collapsed. Wow! This would be fun. He backed away from the building having completed the training.

He then explained I was to complete the task of clearing buildings while he ran back to the home place. His total time away would be approximately an hour, allowing me to finish required tasks and for cleanup to occur.

It was on this day, where I experienced for the first time the realities of leading by example and the consequences of incomplete communication. One could also include the critical step of ensuring understanding of the task at hand by a simple repetition of instructions.

Most likely, Mister Robinson felt he had done an outstanding job leading by example and demonstrating operation of the tractor and the steps involved in destruction. Where we parted ways was what buildings were destined for toothpicks and which were not. I could still see the dust of his pickup leaving the farm when I began the wonton destruction of half the property. I had the biggest smile you've ever seen on anyone's face as I moved from structure to structure dropping the bucket. Because of my inexperience in tractor operations and a hesitancy to go too fast, I was still in action when he returned within the expected time.

If he shifted his pickup into park before he leapt from the cab, he did so all in one motion. I couldn't hear him screaming over the sound of the diesel, but I could see his pale face and mouth moving as he ran toward me waving his arms.

My memory doesn't include an image of him being an athletic man, but he covered the space between us in record time jumping up on the back of the tractor with the grace of a gazelle and it was then his yelling matched the growling of the diesel. I parked and got an incredible dressing down. My joy and fun had all come crashing down faster than the buildings lying in my wake.

Like many leaders, Mister Robinson had done an adequate job teaching operation of the equipment used that day, but had failed to ensure his student fully understood which buildings were to be demolished. I had exceeded my quota by quite a few.

Thankfully, the buildings I took down were intended for destruction, but demolition was to have been done in two ways. Crushing and by hand. Mister Robinson, the thrifty man he was, had intended several buildings to be worthy of repurposing (a phrase not used then, but since made famous). His employee had rendered that impossible.

Lessons to be learned:

Leading by example includes the ability of the person demonstrating to include each step from beginning to end. It also must contain a clear understanding of eventual final outcome. In the businesses I've been a part of over the last five-decades, we've come to understand demonstration in the beginning is fine, but a checklist of each and every step guarantees success and ensures there is no ambiguity of intent or outcome. Left alone, employees who are not fully trained, or communicated with, will destroy buildings you don't want destroyed. They'll do the best they can do, but have no idea what you intended.

It's also a virtual impossibility for most people to understand every step or nuance involved in a process. It's as simple as saying to someone *"How did you get to work today?"*

Well, that question could have dozens of variations based on the person's ability to digest what you've asked them. Frankly, if they were an individual who thrived on detail, they could say. *"Well, my alarm went off at 7:02, I exited my bed on the left side, walked 20 feet to the bathroom…."*

While at Citibank, I occasionally led process mapping efforts. This included creating "swim lanes" representing various departments and the hand-offs and back and forth which occurred. It was an extremely detailed exercise allowing those in charge to eliminate redundancies, reduce time and thereby cost.

It was also a huge eye-opener for those who thought they really truly knew the process being mapped. The question asked above, which most of would have answered by saying *"Tomar south to 69th"* was now being replaced by *"Well, my alarm went off at 7:02..."*

The biggest risk you'll run in leading by example, without some serious training and communication included, is what's being done when you are gone. Like Mister Robinson, there will be many instances when you check back where you'll be surprised, perhaps even disappointed at the progress or outcome.

What are you doing to ensure full awareness of processes; or to what level do you communicate clear goals and expectations?

There's No Such Thing As A Free Lunch

Over the years, I bet I have told this story several dozen times. Frankly, for the first 48 or so years, it seemed funny and odd at the same time. Then, during the last recession, the lesson I learned in my youth came back into focus and made tremendous sense. As I noted in the preface, to not fully grasp all the lessons learned over a lifetime isn't taking full advantage of experiences you've had. Some examples, like this story, will remain latent for decades. Others you've most likely integrated into your being and they have either consciously or unconsciously become a part of you.

Here's the first example where my brain won't allow the memory of the name of the person involved. His farm was located about two or three miles to the east, as the crow flies, from our home on Lake Benton. I was recruited, along with a few other strapping youths, to bale hay.

First, you must know the difference between handling hay and straw bales is fairly significant. Perhaps as much as twenty or thirty pounds depending on the moisture content and density of the alfalfa hay. Second, at around 135 pounds soaking wet back then, I was certainly no Adonis. Throwing and stacking bales was a physically demanding job. The work was done with full denim dress and most likely under a blazing sun. Sleeping well after these full day sessions was easy.

I don't remember the pay scale back then, but "Google" tells me the federal minimum wage in 1974 was $2.00 so I'll go with that. Seems crazy now, but reality back then.

We began our day pretty early and those of us hired to do the work rode on the hay rack while the farmer, our employer, drove the tractor. A steady stream of bales began to be made and came to us from the back of the baler which had a short conveyor.

As was taught, by example, we began placing bales in a particular order to ensure a tight fit necessary for future transport from the field to the farm. The symmetry of this exercise is in itself interesting. Laying a row, stacking the next level at a different angle, then repeating the patterns every other row, or in some other variation had a true purpose. Today, large round bales, hauled eight to ten at a time by semi-trailer trucks have eliminated the need for hand-stacking, and frankly good honest work for teenagers.

So we worked all morning and then it was time for lunch. The wife of the farmer had prepared an ample meal of handcrafted sandwiches, Kool-Aid and cookies. Like most teenagers, especially those who had labored hard for the past four hours, we devoured the lunch before heading out for the second shift.

The afternoon goes by without incident. The last hayrack is brought to the farm, we offload the bales with a few of us on the ground and the remainder in the hayloft of the barn. Funny how off-loading always seemed to go faster than the original process.

I'm sure seeing a light at the end of the tunnel had something to do with it. As we caught our breath, the farmer walked into the house and returned a short time later. It was then, the realities of life and business impacted me. Our employer, to his credit, had constructed a crude handwritten timesheet for each of us, personalized with our first names. Start time, lunch time, resume time, end time.

Much to our dismay, I still remember seeing the disbelief on my buddies faces, and I'm sure it was like looking in the mirror at mine, was the notations of deductions for the break and a charge for lunch. Like those uneducated or ill-informed, I went into the day thinking "Hey, I'll work from 8:00 to 4:00 and bring home $16.00. The farmer had deducted $1 for the half-hour we ate lunch and charged us $2.00 for said meal.

First, let me say no other farmer had ever done this to me before. Second, none of us showed up for Day 2 of fun in the sun. I'm sure we pretty much, in our immature way, pillaged him to all our friends thereby setting up a secret "blacklist" held as sacred by other potential laborers. Now over 40 years later, I look at that day as one of the most pivotal lessons I learned which benefits me the most today. It also may separate me from my liberal friends, whom I love!

Lessons to be learned:

When I look back at the responsibilities I've had, the processes I've observed and the business I help run; it's impossible for me to think of a more valuable lesson I received in life.

It mirrored in some respects the life-lessons my father and mother attempted to pass to their five children as well. You earn what you earn, you make of yourself what you do through effort, not through a gift.

I'll capture a few key points now in an attempt to demonstrate how you may integrate this in your life or business. When I think of you reading this book, it will be fun for me to think about the questions you'll be asking and the thoughts you'll be thinking. The "what if's" for me are always stimulating when considering ways to either make or save money.

A local realtor I know charges a modest monthly rent for shared office space. These professionals are some of the top earners in Sioux Falls, a highly competitive real estate market. First, I think his doing so is smart as they are helping pay for the rent/mortgage. Second, and most importantly, it's that small monthly commitment of money that helps them realize there is no such thing as a free lunch.

When I think back to my Citibank years and the massive (at that time) retention unit where calls from customers who wanted to end their relationship were transferred,

I can't help but think about how much more effective that collective group of people would have been if they had been charged a modest seat fee for their spots on the floor. What are you giving away now as a cost of doing business that you could recoup and perhaps help drive enhanced performance?

As our restaurants moved through tough economic times, we made several decisions critical to our ability to remain viable. With an end goal in mind of making money, and thereby providing a return on investment, making changes was necessary in face of depressed revenues. This was particularly true at Foleys with a decline of travel and entertainment by Fortune 500 companies. That frugality has just now begun to loosen up nearly a decade after the big crash.

As we looked at our business, nothing was off limits for change. Much like the process mapping I had done in the past at Citibank, looking at a step-by-step flow beginning with the products we bought, the employees we had, the facilities we had built, were all considered. One of the expenses we had always absorbed was credit card interchange. Customarily, MasterCard and Visa fees are between 1.5% and 3.0% of sales, with American Express and Discover being outliers with higher rates.

I'm certain you have visited smaller restaurant properties where they only accept cash, or perhaps have a prohibition on Amex or Discover. It's hard in a low margin business to give anything back.

It's even harder in a high volume, multi-million dollar revenue stream business, to see those interchange totals at the end of the year and just accept it as a cost of doing business.

One of the mantras and philosophies of our restaurants had been providing servers their own small business. We paid the rent, we created a remarkable environment, we produced a tremendous product, and then it was up to them to create a memorable experience.

Thankfully, we were extremely successful within our market in creating a legacy of success thanks to the men and women who dedicated themselves to this philosophy. Since we rested on the principle of ownership, we decided to hold back a percentage of server tips to offset the credit card interchange associated with their daily sales. In doing so, they (the servers) were investing in their own success of the evening.

Ironically, we had a server at Tre Lounge tell us a few years ago the practice was illegal. This was brought to her attention while taking a class and articulated by her professor when she mentioned the practice we had employed as policy.

It goes without saying, I wasn't happy this educator spoke without knowledge of the topic or industry. If you are a restaurant owner, or an employer of any tipped employee, do a Google search using key words "withholding credit card fees from a tipped employee". You'll receive a full page of supporting documentation within a millisecond.

So, just as my employer did over four decades ago in providing me my first example of "paying to play", your employees should also know there is no such thing as a free lunch.

In a business where food is all we did, we had several policies in place to mitigate expense and abuse. For example, employee meals all required a ticket. Not doing so, opened us up to hundreds of free (free to them, expense to us) meals and an incorrect calculation on food cost.

I'm probably not in any position going forward to charge any additional fees to servers, but there could be a case made, not unlike the realtor who charges for an office, that they are private contractors. Successful business people explore all avenues, exhaust all ideas and learn from lessons along the way.

John Philip Sousa

Our parents, especially our mother Carol, believed playing a musical instrument of some kind was important. My 4th through 6th grade years included piano lessons. One of my regrets now is not having maintained that skill. In fact, I have no musical ability now having forgotten each lesson. Upon our arrival in Lake Benton, we were greeted by a home visit from the school's Band Director.

I believe his name was Mr. Anderson. I remember him asking me a few questions about what I wanted to play, and I remember telling him drums. Well, he had a pair of drum sticks in his carry bag and he gave me a rudimentary rhythm test.

It wasn't more than a minute or so later when I became the newest Coronet player in the Lake Benton Band! I ultimately graduated into a Baritone and then on to a Sousaphone (Tuba). Ironically, my sister (Cindy), and brother (Jim), became drummers along the way. They also can swim, which is a skill absent in my physical abilities.

Sometime shortly after my debut in band, Lake Benton High employed a new Band Director, Mr. Frost. He was a shorter man in stature, but big in confidence. He clearly loved his vocation and to a greater extent loved marches. As a brass player, you really can't beat a march for participation. I can't recall when it was in my career as a tuba player, but there was a time when Mr. Frost asked me into the office after band practice. The conversation went something like this:

Mr. Frost – *"Randy, are you reading the music and playing those notes?"*

Randy – *"Not all the time."*

Mr. Frost – *"Well, you aren't bad, but I need you to play the music written."*

Randy – *"Okay."*

Truth be told, I would improvise on many occasions. First, this wasn't the thing to do for a perfectionist like Mr. Frost.

Second, my "riffs" may or not have made sense musically or meshed with the rest of my band mates, even though my creative intentions were solid.

In fact, in a band, symphony orchestra, etc. there isn't really any room for improvisation. The only person who gets that autonomy is the person who wrote the music. Sure, there are moments where improvisation exists in Jazz or in other forms of music, when called for, but not in the mainstream. I got the message and towed the line from that point forward.

I ultimately convinced my Mom during my senior year, that my band days were over. I can't remember the logic I used but am sure it had something to do with competing responsibilities of school, extra-curricular activities and a job.

Lessons to be Learned:

Every business has a playbook of some sorts. Not unlike the musical score, there are a set of notes and tempo that needs to be adhered to in order for the band as a whole to sound good. Employees who improvise, or engage in their own creativity, all with good intentions may in fact not be contributing to a unified message or delivery of services.

Yet, a good leader will recognize creativity and find ways to tap into that energy. Perhaps the person will help develop a better mousetrap. Perhaps they'll write the next great march.

As a leader, you'll have an opportunity to exercise a mentality of determining whether you look at the failing as a glass half empty, or glass half full, teachable moment.

Are you a disciplinarian, coach or both? Better yet, when you run a company like I did, you'll I have the opportunity to find out either by luck, or through cause, how many Randy's you have in your band!

Act 1, Scene 1

One of the greatest joys in my life goes back five decades to my involvement in Community Theater and in particular being in plays with my Mother. Lake Benton's historic Opera House was in disrepair in the early 70's and the community rallied around the cause to restore it in several stages. In doing so, they began a long running exposure to theater and other events which continue today.

My mom had a memorable run as a lead in the classic "*Arsenic and Old Lace*," while her oldest son was cast to play Brian Runnicles in the farce, "*No Sex Please, We're British*." There were other performances along the way, but those two opportunities stand out in my memory as highlights. It was the best of times. You really can't put a price on the discipline of learning lines, timing and emotional expression all key components of participation in theater.

I distinctly remember lying in bed before performances, or even right up to curtain time, where anxiety and nerves kicked in and I had a sudden thought that I'd forgotten lines. That will just plain scare you!

One of my favorite stories of being involved in the Opera House, outside of acting, was a play where I volunteered to be lighting and sound. My perch high up in the balcony afforded me a perfect view of the stage below. The performance included many occasions for involvement and other opportunities for down time.

The play progresses and I step outside the booth to an adjacent porch so I may bask in some fresh summer air. I then faintly hear the first lines of a "skip ahead" in dialogue. What was to have been a several minute break in activities requiring lighting or sound, suddenly was shortened by an actor forgetting where they were in the play and beginning a transition to another scene. Included in this was the actor's movement toward a faux switch and the dimming of the lights.

As I stood on the balcony and the voices from below wafted up to me, I suddenly became aware of what was going on. I lurched back in the control booth just in time to catch the movement by the actor to the switch, thereby dimming the lights on perfect queue. Now, is this a big thing? Well, not like life or death certainly, but for the actor involved and the play in general it was.

While it was community theater it also was an attempt by all involved at achieving perfection. It represented the dedication of hours upon hours of learning lines, rehearsing, staging and everything else that went into the production. This was one of those moments where you picked someone else up and moved on seamlessly. Perhaps a theater critic may have had their way with several pages of skipped dialogue, the play continued without skipping a beat.

There's also an interesting parallel between being a leader when comparing plays to television or the movies. Live theater shows preparation, practice and training in real-time, while TV and movies get the benefit of "take two." There are several instances in my life, where I've had to be a bit of a Macgyver and fix things on the fly. I'm sure you have too. Now there's also something to be said about "blowing your lines" in real time, and then recovering. I'll talk later in the book about service recovery and how I believe there's tremendous value in that too.

If you are a parent today, I admire you. The world has provided our youth with so many distractions and competing priorities. There's barely time for the basics, much less extra-curricular activities. Do bands, class plays, debate, community theater exist today? Sure. Are they fashionable or cool? Only you can answer that question when surveying your own children.

 I can tell you with tremendous confidence, the steps my parents took to have me be involved in these activities planted the seeds of teamwork, patience, focus and humility.

Lessons to be Learned:

As an employer, you may want to look beyond grade point average and work experiences while hiring. Peel the onion back a bit and see what outside experiences your candidate brings to the table. Imagine an interview setting where you ask about activities your candidate was involved in during Junior and Senior High. Aren't these in fact the foundation for what they've become today?

Are you surfing the candidates Facebook page to see what type of social citizen they are? If they are immature in their 20's, 30's or 40's (or older like me!) on social media, there's a tremendous chance they aren't able to separate behavior from their personal lives to the one you are seeking as a professional.

When addressing the management team of our company, I often described our restaurants as "the big leagues." We were not Rookie Ball, Single A, Double AA, or Triple AAA (using Baseball analogies), we were in fact the big leagues. Therefore, we needed to perform as if we are on the highest level, the biggest stage.

So, not unlike the actors who participated in those glorious productions of classics at the Lake Benton Opera House, who made a commitment to excellence, we too must maintain that same edge and focus. Doing less denigrates the investment made in the business and diminishes the delivery of end product to the consumer.

Children of the Corn

My athletic years in Lake Benton don't include a lot of personal accomplishment, but I can always say I participated! I still joke today that I have splinters in my butt from sitting on the bench during basketball games.

Lake Benton in the mid 70's was a nine-man football powerhouse. In fact, we won back-to-back State championships with teams that frequently overwhelmed the competition. As mentioned earlier in the book, I was a pretty skinny kid and having no football experience prior to our move didn't help me much when it came to making the squad. After a very brief period of deciding to join the team as a new 8th grader to town, and getting my butt kicked in practice, I decided Cross Country would be my fall sport.

As a Junior and Senior, I had the honor of being Captain of the team. Frankly, I don't remember what my responsibilities were, but I'm sure Coach Jim Roggenbuck (who was also our Principal) had me doing things denoting the position. Well, in this story, I'll share how good a leader I was!

One of our primary training areas then was Lake Benton's scenic "Hole In The Mountain Park." This State park is a hidden gem and at one time also included a tubing hill and the only place within 75 miles where you could ski.

My classmates, Rick Anderson, Craig Gruber and Danny Larsen and I would also frequently tent camp there. The park, in addition to all the fun it provided, became one of my favorite places to run.

I'm not sure whether this event took place during our Junior or Senior year, and I'm unclear who else participated in this particular run, but I know Rick was involved. Coach had given us a running assignment which included a square route running west up Highway 14, turning south on 170th Avenue which was/is a gravel road then east on to County Road 119 back into Lake Benton.

Sometime after instructions were given, and our run was to have begun, there was discussion about cutting corners on our assignment. Rick and I had tremendous knowledge of the park and paths running through it. We, or maybe Rick or I, determined a run through the park and a jaunt through the field on the western boundary would, or could, provide some relief in distance. Basically, an "as the crow flies" route versus taking the established / dictated route.

We probably had a sense, and devious thrill, of "cheating the system" as we took off on the run. I do remember some discussion about how we would pace ourselves knowing the circuit would be shorter. Setting some sort of record for the distance would certainly raise some red flags with Coach. Well our scheme was all well and good until we reached the park's western boundary and found a field of corn stretching basically the length of the section.

To make matters worse, the rows were planted north and south and we had entered from the east. Now if you live in a city, or have never had the opportunity to cross corn from a perpendicular angle, you should know it's not easy! This was what happened to us. Our "time saving" course basically became a major "time sucking" course. We struggled to work our way through the seven-foot high stalks.

After some effort, we found ourselves on the road and way off pace. We were tired from crossing the field and to make matters worse, we had over half the run left. I don't remember how late we were, but I do know we were tardy and clearly off pace. I probably had dirty socks and corn stalks hanging from my shoes.

Our attempt at cheating the system clearly back-fired. I can't remember what we told Coach, but I'm sure it wasn't the truth. I also know he was no dummy and would have easily seen through our ruse. I'm sure he quickly surmised what we had done and to his credit let it go without punishment. Being involved in something wrong, the memory of it, is sometimes punishment enough.

Lesson to be learned:

Every organization with more than two people has a leadership pyramid. Orders are created, communicated, and handed down to a next level for implementation. In my case, as Captain of the team, I was a leader entrusted by the Coach to carry out his orders.

By deviating from the plan I did a couple of things – 1) I sponsored an environment of cheating (more cheating to come in this book!) 2) by altering the plan provided by the leader (Coach), I in fact facilitated an undesirable outcome (we didn't finish our prescribed run within the parameters of time expected. 3) We lied or covered up the truth.

Now no one got killed or hurt in this story. And after all it was only a high school Cross Country training run. But it does say something doesn't it?

As an owner, leader or authority in your company, how many processes, orders or directions are being circumvented by the next levels? How do you know? What methods do you have of auditing and/or monitoring actual performance? It's scary to say you will never really know until your employees show up with corn in their shoes.

Hitting The Wall, Literally!

Leaving for Navy boot camp in August of '77 marked the first time I had flown in any type of aircraft. My ears not popping when we descended into O'Hare was an omen of things to come in my Naval career. I had grown up pretty self-reliant so the drama of landing, finding where I was to go and being herded to Naval Recruit Training in Great Lakes, Illinois wasn't too traumatizing.

The check-in process was not unlike what you'd expect or see in the movies. We had a large packet of papers to hand off and we surrendered anything we had brought with us. I was the first of many assigned to a large barracks, and as the night wore on and other fellow new recruits arrived, we formed the basis for Company 227. When that barracks was filled, an adjacent one was began thereby forming the basis for Company 228. I don't remember how many companies were formed in coming days, but I'm thinking it was over a dozen.

Each company was comprised of at least 70 men. We would all graduate together after training had been completed. The second day represented our full and complete change into recruits. We were all issued dungarees, boots, hats, coats, etc.

We also had our heads shaved. It was around this time a question was posed to the company, "Were any of you in marching band?" I, along with a few others, raised our hands. Presto, I'm a squad leader! What is the connection to band and boot camp? Well, since marching and close order drill would be an important part of our training, having experienced marchers in the front of each line meant, in theory, everyone would follow along. Hence, "Leadership by example!"

Boot camp provided several memorable experiences including firefighting, tear gas, immense chow halls and so much more. The company clearly became closer as the weeks went on and since we were all in the same boat we made the best of what we had.

A significant part of the training had to do with various competitive events. Companies were awarded flags or ribbons denoting accomplishment. As boot camp went on, we began carrying these various flags, including a company flag we designed together, as a sign of what Company 227 represented.

Our company commander, who at that time was probably in his mid-30's, was the source of our leadership. He was good at what he did and we mirrored his enthusiasm along the way.

As we neared the end of training, and the rubber was hitting the road for competitions against other companies, we were scheduled to perform a final close order drill for a numerical score which would have a material and significant impact on our companies' overall place when compared to all others.

The day of the drill, the weather wasn't going to cooperate so we were told of an amended schedule, including being moved inside of a large hall. I'm unsure how big the building was but it's safe to say the total square footage of the giant structure was as big as at least two football fields and then some.

As the march began and we were hitting on all cylinders, our shipmate who was in effect the drum major (leading the company from the front) gave an order to zig left when we should have zagged right. The order resulted in our company marching into a wall. It was a bit like the scene from "Animal House" and the band marching into the alley! There came a point when we couldn't march forward, but everyone marched in place.

I would say the first six or seven rows at least marched into the backs of the person in front of them. An order of "*company halt,*" followed by "*company about face*," was given and we somehow regrouped into the center of the hall to complete our pre-assigned routine.

There wasn't one person in the company who didn't feel devastated by our mistake. When we ended our routine there wasn't much said by anyone, including our company commander, who we naturally wanted to represent to the best of our abilities.

After a short period of time, and following discussion by those who were judging us, we were notified that Company 227 was being awarded the highest score of any company in recent times at Great Lakes Naval Training Center! Following orders, even though they were wrong, which ultimately led to a result non-intended, provided us with this incredible result.

It was perhaps at this time I fully appreciated what the Navy, and the military in general, was all about. When you watch the opening scenes of the movie "*Saving Private Ryan,*" and the soldiers are forging ahead while their buddies are getting blown up around them, it's because they were following orders even though the consequences in their cases was possible death.

Lessons Learned:

The boot camp lesson has stayed with me as denoted by inclusion in this book. Leading others to a result, even when they think the "order" is wrong is an incredibly tough thing to do. As you develop your mission, vision and values and hire personnel to facilitate successful completion, who on your team will follow you even if it means marching into a wall?

If those of you in leadership positions took a hard look at those you've employed what percentage would bail if they disagreed or didn't like the direction they were given? I'm not talking about activities which are illegal, immoral or unethical. I'm talking about the decisions you'll make as a leader which are communicated to those whom you require to follow.

A friend of mine, Jeff Jones, had a long career at United Parcel Service (UPS). He recently mentioned the fact delivery drivers had around 340 steps in the delivery process, including which hand held the ignition key upon exiting a vehicle, in which they could be judged / evaluated when audited for performance.

As a business owner, I often struggled with the amount of individualism I allowed, versus a strict adherence to rules, procedures and "my way." It's this challenge that may in fact be the most demanding of any leader, at any time.

Party Line

This story will not contain names and is uncomfortable to write even though the situation goes back over 30 years. For those who participated, and are reading this book, you will have your own memories and recollections of those go-go days at Citibank. For those who know me and have never heard this story before, let's just say I wouldn't repeat the behavior today. Unless you've been involved in a national start-up on an epic scale, there's no way you could know what it's like. That certainly is no excuse by any means. Those were heady times for me beginning in the fall of 1984.

The incidents of "cheating" I was involved with were all under the direction of one person and spanned a few years. I was directly involved in three distinctly different situations.

I can only assume there were other instances too, but can't say that with any certainty. I think there was some bit of wide-spread knowledge of what was going on, but again that is speculation. The big cop out for many who are caught is always "no one was hurt; no customer was affected." Well, that's B.S. Processes exist for a reason. Circumventing, or wide-scale rigging, has no place in business.

I'll briefly describe one of the three incidents. Perhaps for history's sake, I'll include another in the 2nd edition of what I hope to be a long-running "*Leadership By Example*" series.

It will be captivating for me to sit down and have coffee with you one day and listen to stories you have about your career and times when you knew the fix was in, how you dealt with it then, and lessons you learned which changed you forever.

My first job at Citibank was in a start-up financial services unit called Citibank Financial Accounts (CFA). We were way ahead of our time and had the product / services in test markets around the country. The unit was small enough we actually got to know customers by name which is unique. I started my career as a phone representative, which I really enjoyed.

I later became a second tier manager working under the direction of a Unit Manager. When it was fully staffed, there were around 150 of us in the unit. The experiment ended in 1986 with the project being disbanded and those of us who participated left searching for other opportunities either inside or outside of Citibank.

One of the aspects of the business was an independent unit who monitored phone calls for quality, accuracy and courtesy. This group rated representatives assigning scores. There were various goals for achievement, like 98% against a set scale. Ironically, the quality group used a conference room at the far end of the room where our phone center was situated. Therefore, any time we were go to be monitored, we could see the "police" enter their headquarters, close the door, and everyone knew they had begun.

As you can imagine, word would spread quickly throughout the floor that Quality was monitoring and each person engaged in customer transactions should ratchet up their intensity to ensure all procedures were being followed explicitly.

Well, our Director decided to hedge his bets. He somehow made the phone used to randomly listen to calls in the conference room a "party line." Therefore, the calls being listened to in the quality room, were also available on another phone within the unit. A few of us were instructed to co-monitor calls simultaneously with Quality. When we heard an error or exception to a process being made, we would walk over to the phone representative and gently tap them on the shoulder signifying they should put the customer on hold. It went something like this:

Phone Rep: *"Mr. Jones, I'm going to put on you on a brief hold, I'll be right back."*

Randy: *"You said X, instead of Y. Go back and say Y".*

Phone Rep: *"Mr. Jones, thank you for holding. I apologize, I've researched your account and found that I made a mistake. Please do Y."*

We basically were self-correcting, in real-time, errors made by our phone reps in conversations with customers. Again, customer impact? No, actually better service. Rigging the system? What do you think?

Lessons Learned:

My hospitality career was probably where I most fully appreciated the lessons learned from this experience. With one notable exception (read *"Punchbowl"*). I worked hard to coach our teams into looking at service failures as opportunities to improve. If you don't learn, adapt, change, etc. the mistakes will be repeated over and over again. I also think the Service Industry allows for recovery in a way that provides a heightened level of service.

For example, if you are a server at a restaurant, and you or the kitchen make a mistake, and you go above and beyond in expressing what you've done to correct the error, customers then have a sense you are "all in" and totally focused on their positive outcome. You are engaged.

If our Director would have taken his lumps, training could have been updated, communication could have been improved, etc. Now we all know taking his lumps meant reduced bonuses.

The second lesson here is what does it take to be a "whistle-blower" and do you have it in you to do it? In hindsight, I don't know if I had the courage back then, or if the situation repeated itself would I have it in me today? Would you?

You Can't Keep The Coffee Full

I had made the decision to leave Citibank in the fall of 2005 to join James (Jim) Olson, his son Tim, and Paul Foley to create Pinnacle Hospitality, Inc. Together, we would operate the existing properties of Callaway's and Foleys. Joined a few years later by Tre Lounge. My first day was to be December 1. Responsibilities would include Sales, Marketing and Guest Relations. I've always been able to turn the page and not look back. The same was true about this decision, although the first interaction I had with a customer almost made me regret leaving a prosperous, rewarding, 21-year career.

Jim Olson had received a pointed letter of disappointment in service at Callaway's from Becky Nelson, then the head of what was known at the time as Sioux Valley Hospital. (soon to be transformed into the powerhouse it is now – Sanford Health.) The bottom line was they were on the cusp of leaving the facility for greener pastures. I read the letter the last week of November and agreed to meet with Becky in person as they were to be on the property before the end of the month, a few days before my official start date.

It may seem funny, but in 21-years at Citibank I never met a customer face to face other than an anecdotal incidence on a plane sitting next to someone when they asked where I worked. Such was the nature of this remote business. So meeting Becky would be both fun and yet include a bit of anxiousness.

It is also important to note that Becky's organization was a significant portion of our banquet / meeting business so keeping her happy was important. We met in a hallway during a break in their executive session. Here's the dialogue as I remember it:

"Hi Becky, I'm excited to meet you. I've read the letter you sent to Jim and want to assure you one of the primary reasons I'm joining the company Is to focus on service issues important to you. I'm here to help. Can you describe your biggest issue so I may focus on it immediately?"

"You can't keep the coffee full."

I think this is where the color drained from my face. My inner being was probably like the face Macaulay Culkin made famous in the movie "*Home Alone.*"

Becky went on to describe the fact morning meetings at Callaway's generally included empty coffee pots. If you are in the service industry, you might recognize this as a tipping point for dissatisfaction across the board regardless of what else went right. Becky also made note of outdated audio/visual equipment and a general lack of attention to their needs. I reassured Becky changes would be made and her satisfaction was paramount to me. I basically asked for another chance.

I began my career in the Hospitality business by better understanding the processes for coffee and general service across the board, including wedding receptions, meetings, celebrations, etc. I spent the first year focusing on this important aspect of the company.

Sioux Valley returned in executive session shortly after the New Year and we provided them with a full coffee bar. I leveraged the experiences I had at world-class facilities around the country. Smallish coffee cups were replaced with larger ones. I introduced high quality paper cups with lids for those wanting to take coffee to go. We included several flavored creamer varieties. We enhanced the display to resemble a coffee kiosk. Naturally, we filled air pots non-stop during arrival and breaks. We made ourselves visible. I, as an Operating Partner, provided service thereby "leading by example."

I also wrote letters to key decision makers at Sioux Valley offering my on-going attention to any needs they may have. I made them personal guarantees of my focus and their importance to our business. I also had fun making a difference. To the credit of our team, Callaway's made a habit of being ranked the #1 *"Local Best"* Banquet space in Sioux Falls 7 of the 11 years I was involved.

It was this public affirmation that made the effort worthwhile. Ironically, as we came out of the great recession, when meeting business all but disappeared, Sanford and Avera Health, our two biggest clients in-sourced virtually all of their meetings. They in fact occasionally provide public use of some of their spaces thereby becoming one of Callaway's biggest competitors.

As I neared retirement in the Spring of 2016, I met a customer (ironically from the company my wife is the CEO of – Software Unlimited, Inc.) walking into our banquet kitchen. Customers walking into a service space is always a major red flag. I asked what I could do to help. She said the coffee was empty! I went into the room and found a few scattered air pots and general disorder. De Ja Vu all over again!

Lessons Learned:

I experienced the failure, to success, to failure cycle so prevalent in business today because of turnover at management and staff positions. Because I failed as a leader to fully institutionalize the process of coffee either through rigorous process or observation, we reverted back to our old ways. Not unlike "one hit wonders" in the music business, on-going success takes a lot of energy, focus and attention.

Now, let's turn our focus on the business you own or lead. There was a time when you knew and fully understood key processes. As time has gone by, and employees and other leaders have come and gone, you've lost track of various elements important for success. Haven't you? If you haven't I admire you!

No Punch In The Punch Bowl

While I never tracked a level of accomplishment during my hospitality years, it is safe to say our percentage of satisfaction, based solely on refunds, would have been 99.9%. The through-put of our business numbered in the hundreds of thousands of guests each year and instances of a make-good meal or credit on a banquet experience were able to be counted on one hand each month. That being said, the experience I'm sharing with you is focused on valuable lessons I learned early on which helped shape other decisions I made for years to come.

The Spring of 2006 was an exciting time for me as I was in the process of rebuilding day use of Callaway's through improved processes and I was enjoying my first season of wedding receptions in the facility. It was a blast being behind the scenes as our guests celebrated their day with family and friends. Seeing the room decorated, guests in full dress and the parties rolling into the wee hours of the morning helped shape a feeling of joy I had in the property and the team.

One of the receptions we hosted was for a family from Northwest Iowa who were Dutch Reformed in their beliefs. Therefore, no alcoholic beverages would be served. Since our goal was to accommodate any/all requests within the abilities of our facility and staff, requests such as no booze, special menu items, etc. were welcomed and encouraged.

Over the years, we had a full-time person dedicated to events and each of them had their strengths in dealing with brides, their parents and others involved in planning.

During my time in the business, I always made a point to walk-through every event and often times assisted with plating of the meal, clearing or saying hello and thank you to guests. At receptions, I often congratulated the bride and groom as an "owner." I did the same at the reception in question.

As part of my walk-through, I personally witnessed a significant rush on the punch bowl and a continuous attempt by our staff to keep it replenished. We talked about it behind the scenes. As a former process auditor at Citibank, and one who is big on "first impressions," I rated our service delivery that day, on that one particular part of the process, as a "C."

If you believe in a theory "the customer is always right," (which I don't fully accept, see **Come On Man!**) our customer gave us an "F." Much like the story I shared with you about Becky Nelson and Sioux Valley, the continuously near empty punch bowl at this reception was the tipping point for the mother-of-the-bride to find issue with a series of other service failings (perceived or true) with our staff. She made this known in a pointed letter sent to our Event Director which was then shared with me.

One of her contentions was that "we" (Callaway's) ruined what would have been a special day for her as she basically had to run the event herself.

I don't remember the exact total of the event, but let's say it was $4,000. Her letter asked for a 50% credit. Basically the profit, plus more.

I remember my business partner, Tim Olson, asking me for help in looking at how much credit we should issue and to generate a reply to the guest. My "investigation" included personal observations made on that day, interviews with the Event Director about planning & execution, discussion with staff involved, and lastly a comprehensive and exhaustive review of video images captured from throughout the banquet room including the entry area where the offending punch bowl was situated.

The end of this 20+ hour forensic audit resulted in a "no-fault" letter to our customer denying her request for the credit requested. I was politically correct in my denial, but basically told her the constant rush of guests on the punch bowl was something we shouldn't be held accountable for and therefore, we would issue a credit of a lessor amount. (I can't remember the total but believe it would have been an offer representing the cost of the punch only and perhaps a little bit more).

My letter was soon followed by a pretty fat envelope courtesy of the customer's credit card company. We were being subjected to a 100% "charge back" for the reason of "not as described." Well, now I really got to use the 21-years of experience I had received at Citibank!

I took more time reviewing video and cataloged re-fill times on the punch bowl, number of guests waiting when the punch bowl got empty, counted the number of youth who basically stayed the at the punch bowl drinking, refilling, drinking etc. (p.s. the sherbet based punch served at Callaway's is a 10!). I wanted to make this customer look as bad as I could. Why?

Well some of it was a defense mechanism for our team. Second and perhaps more importantly, the service fail reflected on me too. I've now got about 30 hours into this and my response to the card company was more terse, direct and perhaps even a bit condescending when it came to her (the customer) understanding and expectations versus what our business should deliver.

 I was no longer as politically correct, but I used every bit of my abilities to document, articulate and defend our position. Since the card issuer is in business to defend their customer, now it was "me" against her and them. "Me" lost. A reversal of the entire reception was made by the issuing bank against our account.

Lessons Learned:

A good friend of mine for over 30 years, Scott Christensen, often talks about positive versus negative energy, and opportunity cost while leading. I invested 30+ hours of negative energy on this event making every effort to defend an indefensible position. First, I experienced the punch bowl first hand. Second, I failed to look at the failure in the same light as I did the lack of coffee for Sioux Valley. Why?

Perhaps it was the threat of leaving (Sioux Valley) compared against the request for money back. As I mentioned earlier, there was a large percent of me protecting "us".

I spent the next 10 years focused on creating better future outcomes from individual service fails. I often talked to our team about lessons learned and how to get better. If I spent more than a minute looking at a failure, versus a lot of time looking at the process, for the remainder of my career, it would have been a significant anomaly.

I'm glad I learned this lesson early and frankly to have had a mother who wanted a memorable event for her daughter instead of an empty punchbowl which consumed what should have been one of the happiest days of her life.

Throughout the years, I engaged our team in actions they might have felt as "hokey," but were created to serve a purpose. We journaled service experiences, teamwork and ideas. We brainstormed. We experimented. We had fun.

I think it's a testimony to how we ran our company that employees like Chuck Geurts, April Austin, Nick Rerick, Lisa Jarovski and whole host of others stayed with us. We tried, we learned, we cared.

Janitor By Day, Leader By Night

When I was preparing to leave Citibank in 2005, the majority partner in our company, Jim Olson, asked what my compensation was. By this point in my career it's safe to say I was treated well financially and also had nearly six-weeks off when combining vacation and bank holidays. I also had a tremendous amount of autonomy. The natural inclination when anyone leaves a job for another is to at least make it a lateral move financially. This would be the case for me when I joined Pinnacle Hospitality.

I give Jim tremendous credit as he drew considerably less than I did and had much more at risk in terms of capital. Terms of my employment/partnership included a salary, clothing and car allowances, medical coverage, a cell phone and an employee discount on dining in our properties. As far as I was concerned it was fair compensation when compared to Citibank.

As we neared 2008, the writing was on the wall that things were changing and America was in the beginning stages of the great recession. As managing partners, Jim Olson, Tim Olson and I agreed we would forgo compensation for the upcoming year other than our car allowances, cell phone coverage and medical benefits. Therefore, no paychecks. It was a tough thing to tell my wife who had been more than understanding as our cash out of pocket had steadily increased through capitalizations of the business, and now her husband was going to work for no pay.

How did we do this? Well, not having a family to support helped. Second, I'm an incredible consumer. I have several closets full of clothes. Two sets of golf clubs. Fifty pair of shoes and the list goes on and on. So, I became a non-consumer. I went to a bare-bones lifestyle and frankly it didn't matter one bit. By me shutting off purchasing things I didn't need anyway, we didn't "suffer" at all. This little dose of reality has also come into play again as I've entered semi-retirement. There comes a time when you say "enough is enough." I've reached that point, even though there's that occasional pair of shoes…….

As 2009 began, I did want to be able to pay a loan I had taken to capitalize our share of Pinnacle Hospitality. Previous equity infusions had come from cash on hand, savings, 401K loans, and then finally a bank loan. Therefore, we (my wife and I) were making payments on cash we'd infused as a requirement of our ownership. Naturally, Jim and Tim Olson had to also tap their personal financial resources during recapitalizations.

I wanted to have some earnings if for nothing else to repay my Pinnacle Hospitality loan. I approached Jim and Tim about cleaning Foleys and Tre. I asked what the going rate was and offered to clean both in return for payment. Each location had out-sourced cleaning companies. I cleaned for half the price of these two companies from March to December of 2009.

I began my day by doing the routine janitorial duties necessary to ensuring both properties were ready for business.

It was not a secret I was doing this. Several, if not all, of our staff knew an "owner" of the property was cleaning the toilets. To say I was humbled would be an understatement. To say I was proud of the example I was setting for our team was easy to say even while it was happening.

There is a long list of businesses which have closed over the years for the inability, or perhaps the lack of desire, for significant personal sacrifice. When I speak to University Entrepreneurial Studies classes, I always include the story of my life as a janitor. To not would be like telling half the story or our success.

As we began 2010, we in-sourced our cleaning at both Foleys and Tre. If you visited the former Foleys (sold by Pinnacle Hospitality in the Spring of 2016, name changed to "Morrie's" by new owners in January '17) during that period, it was spotless thanks to the efforts of Chuck and Amy Geurts. Chuck has lead the culinary team there since day 1 and his wife joined him in the cleaning process.

Lessons Learned:

 When I cleaned our properties, I thought of the sacrifices small business owners make in order to ensure their ventures survive. I was by no means a hero during the recession, but doing what I did meant we didn't eliminate any jobs or reduce the salaries of staff who had direct contact with our customers. I think being humbled once in a while, in business or in life is also valuable.

The big lesson we learned was by ultimately transferring these duties to members of our team was they, in turn, took pride in how the facilities looked.

As an operating partner, there was always someone I could approach who was directly responsible as well. It was a win, win for everyone.

We live in a country where so many of our people are on the tit. If I'm ever in a position again where I need to sacrifice in order to ensure our business survives. I'm all in. Would you be?

I Think I Can, I Think I Can, I Know I Can!

I'm the oldest of five children. I was followed by a sister (Cindy), and brothers James, Brian and Barry. The youngest two are identical twins and at 46-years old when this book is being completed, are my "baby brothers." I'm proud of all my siblings. We represent an anomaly in America. Our sister is the only one in the family to have an extended college experience.

The remainder of us have military and/or vocational school educations. We are self-starters. Our mother (Carol) graduated with a degree in education and student taught before she was blessed to give birth to the author. She returned to the workforce later in life when the twins were nearly out of high school.

Our father was an Army veteran, who worked very briefly at Boeing in the mid 50's and then began what could only be described as a remarkable career at Land O' Lakes with many promotions and responsibility changes.

When I enlisted in the Navy in November 1976, I did so with the intent of using the G.I. Bill to go to college upon discharge. I did in fact enjoy G.I. Bill benefits, albeit at a private broadcasting school in Minneapolis, Brown Institute. "Brown" has long since closed which is a shame given their incredible legacy of training some of the best broadcasters in the country.

My passion for music, the fact I was economically spoiled coming out of the Navy, and a fear of committing four-years to education were all factors in my selection of Brown. The school was an 11-month crash course in radio, TV and voice work. I lucked into a job after graduating in 1982 at KLOH-AM in Pipestone, Minnesota thanks in part to my friend John Veire, a graduate of Lake Benton's class of '76. John made me aware of a job available at the station and I pursued it.

I took a sales job as a way to get inside the station with the full knowledge of high turnover among on-air radio personalities. I felt if I got in and waited, I'd be on-the-air someday. This came true sometime in 1983 and "Randy Lee" was born. I wasn't very good. I'm sure not the talent of a few friends who remain at the station today, Mylan Ray and Bernie Wieme. They were and remain true professionals.

I had a few other strikes against me. I met a girl and my buddy Matt Yseth "coerced me" to play golf almost every day. The combination of those two, combined with a lack of motivation and full commitment to sales goals, ultimately led to me being encouraged to do something else by the station's owner Wally Christensen. I was one of those employees who fire themselves. Wally helped me with an incredible life lesson. Don't do anything you aren't completely passionate about. I've never forgotten his well-timed kick in the butt.

So now I'm in the job market and Citibank is hiring! Boy are they ever. The company was growing leaps and bounds and staff by the hundreds were joining the company each month. When I began in November of '84 there were fewer than 1,000 people in a facility which would ultimately cap out at 3,200. There were less than 1,000 of us in what would by the end of my career include upwards of 60,000 people throughout the world tied to Citibank's credit card business. Incredible.

When Citibank Financial Accounts (CFA) was to be shuttered and disbanded, I caught a break. Thanks to Jane Kuper who worked in Human Resources at Citi, I became a candidate to join a one-year Management Associate Program designed to bridge staff into management. I was the only candidate in the history of the program at the time to enter the program without an undergraduate degree.

To her credit, Jane saw my military experience (I remained in the U.S. Naval Reserve from my discharge in 1981 to 1990) as representative of the type of people they were looking for. From that point on each step I took in my career was the result of hard work, effort and an appetite to grab opportunities when they arose. Such was the case in the Spring of 1990.

I took a phone call one day from Long Island City, New York. It was from Colleen Mooney. I knew Colleen from her time in South Dakota in both the Correspondence Unit and the aforementioned CFA. She had called for Becky Ingalls, who was my supervisor (need to add her to the list of influential women I worked with!). Here's how the conversation went:

"Is Becky there?"

"No, actually Becky is on maternity leave. Can I help you?"

"I was calling to see if she would be interested in moving to Long Island City."

"Well, I can't speak for her, but I would have to think having a baby recently would most likely result in a "no" answer."

"How about you?"

"I can think about it."

In the next few months I got engaged, got married, transferred and began a three-year run in Long Island City, New York!

I was a real fish out of water now. Colleen, Myra Koutzen and perhaps a few other people had made the quantum leap from Operations to Front Office. I was the latest on this list and at this point in history, nearly 30 years later I may have been the last. It was a bridge most people didn't want to cross. Not only was it New York City, but it was corporate versus the rest of the company.

I remember my interviews prior to moving and my education, or lack of it, was discussed but again experience and enthusiasm allowed me to move forward. When asked by co-workers, and it was rare if I was, I said I went to "Brown." This was true, even though all my co-workers who went to Yale, Columbia, Penn State, etc. never caught on. Thank God I was never pressed into answering to a true Brown University alum!

The rest they say is history. I had remarkable experiences in New York. Both personally and professionally. My career took on a whole new trajectory and I moved back to South Dakota in 1993 with a new found sense of pride and accomplishment.

For the next decade, I took chances and pushed the boundaries of my abilities through promotions and lateral transfers. I ran employee communications, joined corporate audit, embarked on a special project cataloging every business measure, led a massive training effort when AT & T's Universal Card business was acquired by Citi, and so much more.

I managed my career the best way I knew how.

Lessons Learned:

My story is not unique in comparison to millions of others in our country who decide to forgo college. Having a company willing to overlook and/or appreciate experience in lieu of a degree is admirable. I'm pretty sure people like Colleen, Myra and Jane went to bat for me and are significant reasons I had the opportunities I had. I'm humble enough to know I didn't do it on my own.

There's a thread which runs through my life, beginning with my father who earned his way, which allowed me to become who I became. It wasn't always rosy. I cleaned a few toilets along the way!

We are in a unique time in history. The generation who is graduating now is an entitled group. They haven't wanted or needed much in their lives. Therefore, the fact they are graduating from college and are either unemployed or under-employed is troubling for them. Starting on the ground floor, or paying dues, is virtually unheard of anymore.

Vocational or Trade schools are often looked at in disdain and as a poor second or third choice. The military? I don't know of anyone who looks at the military as a terrific way to broaden your horizons and gain real-life skills. To their credit, my friends Matt & Cathy Yseth's sons have figured this out!

The other significant change in our country is the end of long-term careers. New York was a perfect example for me of the in-and-out revolving door of talent. Job jumping is the new norm. My father's 35-year career is such an anomaly now.

Some of this has to do with company's contracting as well. I'm sure many of my Citibank brothers and sisters who were downsized the last decade didn't want to have that be their end. But it was and is a way of life. Outsourcing, off-shoring and other new phrases rule the day.

In the end, only you can manage your career. Your ability to lead through various administrations, ownerships and other regime changes is key to your survival. How are you doing?

When It's Time To Say You Were Wrong.

My brief supervisory experiences in the Navy didn't afford me the opportunity to hone any coaching or corrective action skills. I, most likely, was the receiver versus the giver back in those days. At Citibank, I was introduced to a set of established corrective action steps related to performance, behavior or other important aspects of conformity.

One of my earliest memories of pushing back on the system came on a Saturday morning while sitting with Jean Collins in the bank's Correspondence Unit. Jean, along with another Jean (Reed), also had tremendous influences on my professional life over the years. It's safe to say I was influenced and molded more by women than men during that 21-year career.

Jean was encouraging me to put a representative on my team on corrective action for missing productivity standards. The unit had a series of them tied to various actions we took on behalf of customers. Address and name changes being examples. At that time, I was an entry level Unit Manager and my team consisted of all women. Jean was the next layer above. I remember the conversation well and it has continued to frame my beliefs on corrective action ever since. Here's a summary of the talk:

Jean: *"You need to put Sally on verbal warning for missing standards."*

Randy: *"I'm hesitant to do that as I don't know if I've done enough to help Sally achieve the goal."*

Jean: *"Well, do a better job."*

There were probably a couple of forces at work here. First, I most likely wanted to avoid the confrontation which accompanies corrective action. Second, I truly believed then I may have been lacking in prior attempts to assist Sally.

If there's a person in the world who enjoys meting out corrective action. He/She is a true narcissist. As I progressed through my career I found various ways to make the process easier and better.

When I joined the hospitality industry and was up-close and personal with the people who created and served the fruits of our labor, I did so wanting to show them my abilities and my "like" for them. In fact, there came a time when I had somewhat befriended a line cook at Callaway's.

Jim Olson pulled me aside one day and told me to not become too close to our employees as there may come a day when I'd be firing them. Well, during my hospitality operating phase, I managed to keep my like for people, with a bit of distance ensured allowing for those discussions to occur. In the end it's all about mutual respect. You respect them, they respect you. What happens in-between is business.

It's hard when you are working in the trenches alongside them to not get close. It is why perhaps top-tier CEO's, COO's or others in corporate America stay in their offices and find it so easy to downsize and eliminate.

For me, when there was capital at risk, or business could not support having the number of people we had, then it still was always about the business. Jim Olson helped teach me that. After all, the payroll we had was in fact our/my money.

Over my years at Pinnacle Hospitality, I had to fire several key people, who at the time they were hired seemed like they were capable, willing and key components of the business. It was their performance which ultimately led to them not being retained.

When dealing with our staff, which occurred after our next-tier managers had done what they could, or I was asked to intervene, I liked to rely on repeatable dialogue consistent from employee to employee. Case in point:

"Chris, I've got 150 employees and your name comes up way to often. You need to make sure I hear your name less for bad things, and more for good things." Short and to the point.

Corrective action actually became easier along the way and in the end, employees who were discharged from Pinnacle Hospitality frankly ended up doing it to themselves just like I did at KLOH. A familiar phrase when I became involved in termination discussions was *"you don't give me any choice."*

I don't know if you feel like this, but it really is the case. A business that has set parameters for behavior, accomplishment and responsibilities must simply reduce the amount of gray by ensuring black & white. Once you allow something for one, you've basically allowed it for all.

You may ask if working in a corporate setting versus running your own enterprise has significant differences when it comes to Human Resource administration. The biggest difference is time. Where a corporate structure may include many steps, at Pinnacle Hospitality we choose to "hire slow and fire fast." Offending actions were routinely handled within a very short amount of time.

We would discharge on the spot if the infraction was serious. This was done to ensure every person on our team knew his/her role was vital to daily operations.

Lessons Learned:

Jim Collins coined the phrase, *"who's on your bus?"* as a metaphor for who you've surrounded yourself with. It's a nice easy way to look at things. In close quarters, it's easy for leaders to get cozy with those who work for them. It's easy to become someone's "friend." However, in the end, you have to make decisions which safeguard, protect and defend policy. Acting quickly, decisively and with consistency can actually be morale builders within an organization. Those who play by the rules always enjoy the fact they are playing the game right.

Every business, regardless of size, should have an employee handbook detailing the various guidelines for employment. Owners of the company should be held responsible for the same rules as their staff. We had a general policy that if you cashed a check from the company every two weeks you abided by the same exact rules.

There was no deviation and I reminded myself of that often when it came to my own behavior and actions both inside and out of the company. Not having done so would have been hypocritical.

Where's The Dress?

I'm by no means a pragmatist or a deep thinker. In our house, I leave that to my math major and computer science minor wife. I'm a free-thinker and at times (like perhaps my investment in the restaurant business) a whimsical risk taker. What I do respect is process. In fact, while at Citibank I reveled in the opportunity to create wall-sized process flows.

So, my years spent in Corporate Audit at Citi were some of my most memorable experiences. I was drafted, mainly because no one wanted to do it, into a situation where I once lead a significant portion of Citi's credit card businesses "self-assessment" audit program.

There were several instances and experiences which have stuck with me over the decades since they occurred. A time when my good friend, Thorner Harris and I, were in Cheyenne, Wyoming at a telemarketing agency and their representatives during the opening meeting gushed about how they espoused Citibank's values to their employees engaged on the business.

In fact, they said they even documented it on new hire orientation paperwork. We, in turn, asked for a roster of employees and highlighted every seventh one, and asked for their orientation paperwork. This is when the color drained from the face of the H/R person, as the claim had most obviously been exaggerated and most likely had significant gaps.

Another trip resulted in yours truly climbing a ladder to inspect possible options for entry into a print shop and found an open roof hatch directly above the shredding bin, which by the way was never shredded. When asked by their facility manager what I had been doing on the roof, I returned his question with a question of my own as to why they had made it so easy for identity thieves to enter their facilities.

A similar situation occurred on another trip, when I was visiting a site and their manager took me outside the facility to show off their newly double-tinted windows, thereby making it *"impossible"* for anyone to look in. On this visit, I made a point of going back to the facility unannounced that evening to take pictures of all the screens and customer data available to be seen from the outside when the entire room was lit up with no blinds closed (basically the entire first floor).

One other time, I was in Nova Scotia (that was a remarkable trip. Seven northern Canadian cities in six days). I had arrived early because I was unsure of total driving time from the hotel to the facility.

As I sat in my car waiting for the appointment, a side-door to this secure facility opened and dozens of people streamed out to smoke cigarettes. As they began their return into the building, I integrated myself into the mass and had a nice walk-around from screen to screen looking over the shoulders of the telemarketers and writing down customer data.

I then made my way to the front-desk to wait for my host. Needless to say, the first five minutes of our visit was interesting!

But perhaps the one experience, containing the most fun and most to learn from, happened at an Advertising Agency in mid-town Manhattan. Bill Reidy and I were assigned to go to the agency as there were questions on billings made and the veracity and accuracy of how much was being paid and for what. These forensic reviews were stimulating and really opened my eyes to attention paid, at various levels, by authority figures within Citi. It's a lesson easily transferred to virtually any business.

So imagine paper boxes filled with invoices, emails and other documentation tied to a print, TV or other campaign done by the agency on behalf of Citibank. This is what Bill and I looked through for about three days. When we needed more information, our contact at the agency (most likely a lower, or at most mid-level staffer) would retrieve what we asked for.

There was a general tendency at most agencies to give less and hope there wouldn't be more! One of the campaigns we reviewed had to do with Citibank's novel campaign related to earning points. There were TV commercials, large billboards, magazine ads, etc. that had a tag similar to this, *"Did he do it for you, or for the points?"* It was a successful, catchy campaign.

As Bill and I dug through the invoices, several discrepancies and failure to follow policies were being found. One of their staff members had a proclivity to take "black cars" home rather than take a subway, train or other method of travel. Policy allowed for this, but only if it was associated to late night work. Other miscellaneous unauthorized expenditures also surfaced along the way. It was while reviewing sheet after sheet of expenses associated with a TV commercial and associated photo shoot, that we came across an interesting item.

Among line after line, on dozens of invoices, all being denoted as "rented or leased" by the agency, we came across a purchase of a wedding dress. Rent, rent, rent, rent, lease, lease, lease, purchase. Interesting. First, as one who didn't know what things cost in general, you really had your eyes opened too what it took to cater in mid-town Manhattan, or what a photographer's hourly fee is, etc. But then there was this purchase of a wedding dress.

So, as was protocol, we summoned our contact and briefly described the process we were using reconciling invoices to approvals and the fact this particular activity had a series of rentals, leases, invoices to professionals, etc., but also a purchase of a wedding dress. Here's how this went,

Bill Reidy: "*Where's the dress?*"

Agency Representative: "*What do you mean?*"

Bill Reidy: "*Well, if Citibank paid for the dress, it's our dress.*"

Agency Representative (after a brief moment and a quizzical look): "*I need to follow-up on this.*"

After a short while, a person with whom we had no prior contact arrived in our room and we repeated the same conversation with her. There was clearly a bit of surprise on her part, First, I believe because what we had found in this situation was a result of a purely random sampling of business they had conducted on Citi's behalf. Second, I think she was surprised at the thoroughness of our review. We made a point to ask about the black car use too. When given a box full of all kinds of materials, it takes a keen eye to spot abnormalities.

I often used my audit experience in the hospitality business. I used the sense that small issues often led to larger problems. In this audit's case, it was the general lack of oversight on the entire business and the steady drip, drip, drip of unauthorized expenses which kept our attention.

In the end, the dress was never explained or returned, but the total if memory serves me right, was somewhere around $17,000. So you've read this and now you're probably asking what the end of this story is.

Well, in this particular audit, and as a result of other programs we looked at as a result of lack of oversight, Bill and I wrote a report listing the realistic opportunity, based on our contract with the agency, to recover nearly $200,000 against multiple millions paid to the agency.

Our overarching conclusion was those at Citi charged with safeguarding and protecting the bank's assets were either asleep at the wheel or negligent in their duties.

It was our job to report and recommend, it was to those who received the report to act. Bill and I both agreed no action would be taken, but we never knew for sure.

Lessons Learned:

There's not many businesses in the world who don't either outsource or delegate somewhere along the line. In our hospitality business I know for sure, and with tremendous confidence, there was money spent or squandered which clearly would have been considered unauthorized.

Part of running a company is "cost of doing business" involving employee theft, mistakes, etc. Any restaurant or bar owner will tell you keeping tabs on everything is the fine-line between success and failure. How simple is it for a bartender to over-pour to his/her buddies?

Not unlike other examples in this book, it's not just about the process. It's about the ability to actually monitor and measure the processes on an on-going basis. In some cases, the amount of diligence may in fact be more expensive than the loss. One of my wife's family's closest friends, Dan Parrish, once commented his wife had lost her credit card. When I asked if he had closed the account, his reply was, *"No, they spend less than she does!"*

One of the biggest things I had to accept, and reconcile almost daily, was what I was willing to "*put up with,*" as a business owner. If you are seeking perfection, within an imperfect world, what will set you off? Manufacturing businesses who seek excellence will often talk about six-sigma. This is most simply defined by 3.4 defects per million transactions. 3.4!

So now you're a leader and you start to look around at what you're responsible for and you think of the processes you've created, or the ones your responsible to monitor, and you start to shake your head at what is in fact reality.

I've had the opportunity to share my experiences in the hospitality business with various groups of businesses and classes. I like to use this example as something representative of the little things which help shape opinion. The story goes like this:

"Imagine it's your birthday and you are being treated to dinner at a restaurant you've always wanted to go to. It's going to be a special night and you spend the day in excited anticipation of the evening. As you near the front door of the restaurant, you notice the receptacle for cigarette butts is overflowing.

Your eyes are also drawn to the fact the large glass doors are smudged and most likely haven't been cleaned for a while. Immediately upon entry you make a decision to use the restroom. Again, clearly a lack of focus by ownership as there are towels on the floor and one of the stalls is inoperable.

After coming out and into the lobby you see a teenaged hostess texting on her phone oblivious to your party's arrival. What are your impressions now?"

As a leader responsible for vendors, contractors, or your businesses processes how are you stacking up on all the small things which make a difference. What are you letting go, or putting up with?

Come On Man!

The first edition of "Leadership By Example And Other Terrible Ideas" is going to end with one of the most pressing issues facing leaders today and into the future. Social Media. As a small business owner, I had to address this head on. It wasn't fun.

First, I'm a huge believer in feedback. When I talked early on about fixing the Chili, I took each similar opportunity as a way to succeed and a distinct competitive advantage. The lessons learned early from the reception at Callaway's still resonate with me today. Yet, I'm troubled by a global process whereby a minority of consumers can dictate, articulate, stimulate, or suppress business.

Some leaders have told me they take the results *"with a grain of salt,"* or let unsatisfactory reviews roll-off their backs. They are different people than I am. The veracity and honesty of *"Angie's List", "TripAdvisor", "Yelp", "Urban Spoon",* and myriad host of other sites available are doubtful.

Several recent news articles have highlighted the easy way in which the ratings may be manipulated. All that said, the sites and their outcomes intended, or un-intended, are a way of life.

A few years ago, I got caught up in a Facebook battle. The manager on duty at the downtown Hilton Garden Inn, a location Pinnacle Hospitality was contracted to run food and beverage operations called me almost immediately after it happened.

Our managers did this as a matter of routine so I would become informed, and prepare as necessary, for potential blowback and/or corrective action. As mentioned earlier, the times this occurred were actually rare in comparison to incredible amount of throughput we had. This particular incident involved parents, their small child, and utensil pounding damage to a table. Long story short is the father posted some less than favorable remarks on Facebook which were then countered by yours truly.

The episode drew the attention of local media and put all of us involved in a bad light. At one time in my life I learned a lesson. "Write It. Read It. Delete It." I broke my own rule that night. My leadership desire to defend our manager was hasty and put our relationship with the hotel in jeopardy.

I approached less than favorable reviews differently after that. I didn't do any responses at night. I slept on everything. My comments became much more politically correct and usually provide an offer for additional feedback sent directly to me.

I did my best to accept any/all feedback on facility, service or quality of the product. It goes without saying no one enters into a day with failure in mind. Each of us regardless of our position as leader or follower is driven to do the best we can do. Failure to do so means certain failure in the long-term.

However, in a viral world, where there never seems to be any retractions, each leader is left open to be second guessed, ridiculed or worse. At what point may you defend yourself versus taking it? It will be interesting to see how this part of our culture evolves in the next decade.

Lessons Learned:

I don't think you have to completely buy-in to the "customer is always right" philosophy. Doing so may often be tempered by a decision you've made in the best interests of your company, your employees, profitability, etc. Compromise and effective communication will go a long way in smoothing the waters of dissatisfaction. Feedback of all kinds, while invaluable, may not always constitute change.

As a leader, if you have not faced a social media challenge, are you prepared to? What steps would or could you take to offset a full-on blitzkrieg of your business?

Back in the Citibank days, our phone centers would see significant spikes in call volumes after a particular "*Oprah*" or other talking head show focused on the credit card industry.

I remember receiving, and later authoring, talk-offs used by thousands of call center employees.

In our hospitality company, we would do our best to communicate all news, good and bad, before it hit the press. Having our staff know first was important to us. In the Facebook event, once I knew it was going to be story, I immediately called my contact in the company which owned the hotel.

I also sent heartfelt apologies to several key people. It was my hope they accepted my actions for what they were – an error in judgement. I also sat face-to-face with the employees of the restaurant and apologized for what I had done and the light being shined on all of us.

Leaders make mistakes. Leaders who are humble, admit error and learn are better leaders because of it. Can you imagine a world where leaders, politicians and others with grand influence made amends for mistakes versus running from it and / or covering it up? That would certainly be something to see and experience.

I'm not immune to feedback! This book has undergone a rigorous editing process. If you find any typographical errors let me know and they will be fixed.

Thank you for riding along. Look for the next edition soon!

About the Author.

Randy Derheim is a semi-retired executive who resides in Sioux Falls, South Dakota with his wife of 26 years, Pam. Randy's passions include music, golf, public speaking, writing and friends. His novel *She Said, "One"*, was published in 2012.

Over the past decade he has been a presenter and guest lecturer at the University of South Dakota, South Dakota State University and Dakota State University. One of the biggest joys of his life was providing the 2014 Commencement Address at what would then be known as Brown College, the successor to his beloved Brown Institute. It was the last address given as the school closed prior to another graduation (not his fault!)

In January 2017, Randy began as a "Food Ambassador" at Avera-McKennan Hospital in Sioux Falls where he finds joy, humility and purpose in serving food to patients two days a week. Randy feels blessed to have the life he has and relishes each day as if it were his last.

Randy may be reached most easily though his consulting company's email address: bellcowconsulting@gmail.com

Made in the USA
Lexington, KY
11 April 2017